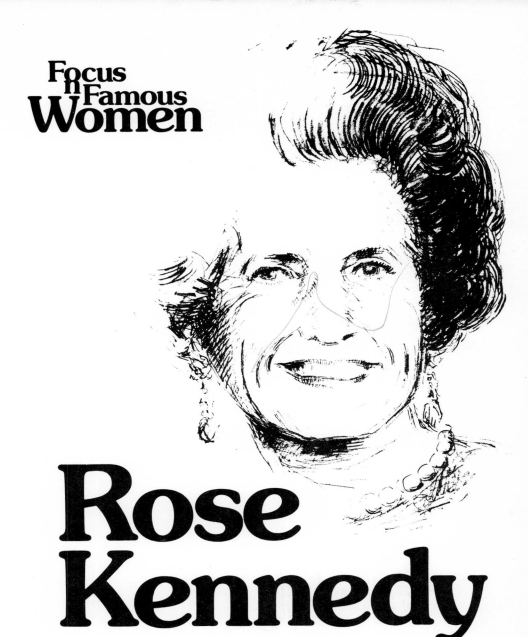

Focus
n Famous
Women

Rose Kennedy

No time for tears

8422

CAROL BAUER CHURCH

Greenhaven Press, Inc.
1611 POLK ST. N.E.   MINNEAPOLIS, MINNESOTA 55413

PHOTOGRAPHIC CREDITS

Boston Globe Photos: Cover, 2, 40, 43, 70, 71, 72, 75, 79.
Wide World Photos: 5, 8, 19, 20, 27, 29, 33, 42, 45, 46, 48, 49, 54, 60, 76.
UPI: 12, 14, 16, 18, 21, 23, 24, 25, 31, 35, 38, 51, 53, 56, 58, 62, 64, 66, 67, 68, 73,
74.

© 1976 by Greenhaven Press, Inc.

ISBN 0-912616-44-X

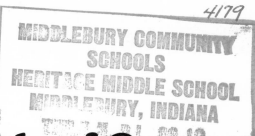

Table of Contents

Rose Kennedy

No time for tears

Introduction

Today, in Hyannis Port, Massachusetts, Rose Fitzgerald Kennedy lives a quiet life. She walks along the beaches of the Atlantic Ocean thinking over days of the past. Her house seems quiet now.

Tragedy took four of nine children from her: Joe in Europe during World War II; Kathleen in Europe, in 1948; John in Dallas, Texas, in 1963; and Bobby in Los Angeles, California, in 1968. Her husband Joseph died after a long illness in 1969.

Four daughters, Rosemary, Eunice Shriver, Jean Smith, and Pat Lawford, and one son, Ted, are very much alive. They and twenty-eight grandchildren carry on the flame of life.

With her faith in God and in His goodness, Mrs. Kennedy feels close to all her loved ones. She believes that someday her family will be together again.

Hoping in life hereafter, the eighty-five year old woman lives her life in peace.

She has no time for tears.

1

The Fitzgeralds and the Kennedys

The great Irish famine of the 1840's brought Thomas Fitzgerald and Patrick Kennedy to the New World. To avoid starvation which was taking thousands of lives, they left their beloved County Wexford, Ireland.

The trip to America on crowded ships took almost two months. Only the strongest and healthiest weathered the terrible living conditions aboard ship to arrive safely on the shores of the land of plenty.

Making their homes in and near Boston, Massachusetts, the Irish found they were not welcome. They were considered the scum of the earth by the original settlers who had little use for the newcomers. After all, the Irish were poor, ignorant peasants, lacking in culture and the niceties of upper society. The Irish possessed a great deal of faith, however, together with dogged determination.

Thomas Fitzgerald met and married an Irish lass, Rose Mary Murray, while Patrick Kennedy met and married Bridget Murphy. Both young couples set to work building their futures and their fortunes.

4

Outgoing "Honey Fitz," Mayor of Boston, with his daughter, Rose

But time was short for the Fitzgeralds. Both Thomas and Rose Mary died in their thirties leaving nine sons, including John Francis, the third oldest. It was this third son who took it upon himself to keep the family together by providing for his six younger brothers until they could take care of themselves.

When John first saw Josephine Hannon, it was love at first sight, and he knew she would be his love forever. He married her, and within a year, on July 22, 1890, they were blessed with their first daughter, Rose Elizabeth. Because John knew of no female relatives in Ireland or in America, he considered the birth of a daughter a first class miracle. She was to remain his favorite daughter throughout his whole life.

John Francis Fitzgerald was a man of great physical and mental vigor. Seldom did he give his body or mind a rest. Because he lived in Boston where history had been made during Revolutionary War days, he used every chance to make his six children aware of their American heritage. He and the family spent many hours and days touring the historic sites where plans for freedom were made and carried out.

Dark-haired Rose grew very close to her father. Like him, she developed an open and interested mind at an early age. And like him, she developed the habit of clipping news items and notes to curtains, bulletin boards, and lapels, so she could remember something important.

John Fitzgerald or "Honey Fitz," as he came to be known, was active in politics, organizing the Irish Catholic vote in a society which was largely English and Protestant. He soon became the only Catholic and the only New England Democrat in the United States Congress. Politics kept him on the run, and he spent little time at home.

Josephine Fitzgerald was a reserved woman who seemed to contrast the out-going qualities of her husband. Where he loved being the center of attraction, she avoided public life. Because of Josephine's natural shyness, her daughter Rose often took her place during speeches and other ceremonies. Josephine was most careful with money, demanding that each penny be accounted for. This quality was passed on to Rose.

From her parents Rose received what she considered the most precious treasure of all: a deep belief in and love for the Catholic Church. Catholicism was the faith of her fathers, and she found its roots were sunk deeply in her heart and mind.

Rose grew up in a lovely home where she received more than her share of attention. She enjoyed wearing fine clothing and fashionable hats. Horse and buggy trips, tree climbing, games with her five brothers and sisters, and family celebrations were all part of her girlhood days.

**Wedding day of Rose Elizabeth Fitzgerald and
Joseph Patrick Kennedy, October 7, 1914**

By the time of her graduation from Dorchester High
School, her father was mayor of Boston, having defeated a
candidate from an old Boston family. His victory was no
small accomplishment for an Irishman. When "His
Honor" presented a diploma to his daughter, Rose, the
youngest girl graduate in the school's history, newspapers
carried the story and photograph on the front page.

After graduation, Rose and her sister, Eunice,
accompanied their parents to Europe. The girls remained
for a year at a convent boarding school in Holland where
they learned all the homemaking skills. They also learned
music, art, languages, and a new appreciation for their
religion.

Returning home to the States for a vacation, Rose and
Eunice found their mother had missed them more than
they had realized. They did not return to Europe for more
schooling. Although she hoped to attend Wellesley, her
father had his way; and Rose finished college at
Manhattanville, New York, graduating in 1910.

On January 2, 1911, Boston newspapers carried these
headlines:

*"Debutante at Reception. Miss Rose E. Fitzgerald,
Gowned in White, Receives More than 500 Friends
at Mayor's Home."*

A large photo of Rose and her mother covered half the front page.

During her high school and college years, Rose had been secretly dating a young man named Joseph Patrick Kennedy, grandson of Patrick Kennedy who had come from County Wexford, and son of Patrick Joseph Kennedy and Mary Hickey. Young Joe Kennedy's father, ''P. J., '' and Rose Fitzgerald's father, ''Honey Fitz,'' were acquaintances, if not friends. Both were extremely active in Boston politics. Whatever the reason for the secret dating, Rose and Joe soon found they were in love.

Ambitious young Joe knew what he wanted, and by age twenty-four, he was probably the youngest bank president in the country. With that achievement, he finally convinced his future father-in-law that he was good enough for Rose and won her hand in marriage.

The wedding took place on October 7, 1914, with Cardinal O'Connell of Boston officiating in his private chapel.

As the Twig is Bent

Joe and Rose, living in a small house at 83 Beals Street in a suburb of Boston called Brookline, were delighted at the birth of their son, Joseph P. Kennedy, Jr., on July 28, 1915. Less than two years later, John Fitzgerald Kennedy was born on May 29, 1917. The two sons were bound to be friendly rivals from their earliest years.

Next came Rosemary in 1919, and Kathleen in 1920. Four children arrived in less than five years, and the family outgrew its first home. It moved a short distance to 131 Naples Road in Brookline where the next three children, Eunice, Pat, and Bobby, were born.

Rose was often seen walking her newest baby in a buggy with two or three toddlers straggling along behind. They would stop at the neighboring church to make a visit and say a few short prayers. Rose wanted her children to know that religion was something for every day, not just for Sunday, and that God was an ever-present friend. She was a proud and happy mother, working to raise her children as perfectly as possible.

Joe was building up his own businesses and fast becoming a genius with money. His work took him away from home on many business trips. Rose accepted his absence from the home because she knew he had his work to do, and she had hers. Their jobs were clearly defined.

Rose with five children, (left to right) Eunice, Kathleen, Rosemary, John, and Joseph Jr., in 1921

''As the twig is bent, so does the tree incline,'' Rose believed. She knew the children's early years affected the future direction of their lives. Being a mother required her best efforts. Unlike most mothers, she had all the help and money she needed, but she still had to plan and supervise the activities of her children.

The last two children, Jean and Ted, were born after the family moved to New York City in 1926 to be closer to Joe's work.

The Kennedy front porch was large enough to be divided up so the children could have their own private play areas. They could watch the activity of the city from the safety of their porch while at the same time breathing in fresh air.

During the early years Rose began using index cards to keep records of her children's dental appointments, doctors' appointments, religious events, height, weight, and dates she wanted to remember. In later years her file card system made her famous as the main organizer of the Kennedy household.

Joe and Rose aboard ship as they returned from a trip to Europe

Family meals of the Kennedys have also received much publicity. Both Joe and Rose wanted their children to have their own ideas and be able to express them clearly. News items were posted on a bulletin board placed near the dining room. Each child was expected to read and be able to make some comment or ask some question about what he or she read. Conversations were, of course, lively as the children tried to outdo each other and even heckled each other. But through this activity, they challenged each other to grow in knowledge and clearness of expression.

To prevent the older children from drowning out the younger ones, a separate table was set where talk was suited to younger minds. The smaller children were usually joined by their mother at supper.

Nightly phone calls came from ''Daddy'' away on business. Each child lined up, one by one, to have a quick word with him. One thing Joe always asked of his children was this: ''Win!'' ''Don't come in second or third,'' he would say. ''That doesn't count, but WIN!'' He wanted his children to use the gifts and talents they had received and do as well as possible. His children told him of their successes and disappointments. He often comforted them with these words, ''That's the best thing that could have happened to you.''

(Left to right) Edward, Jeanne, Robert, Patricia, Eunice, Kathleen, Rosemary, John, Rose and Joe

When the children were young, Rose's business was the family, and Joe's was providing money for present and future needs. From the very beginning, they worked together as a closely-knit unit to reach their goals.

3 Chapter

Glamorous Years

In 1929 the stock market crashed. Banks went broke, and most people lost their money. Jobs were very scarce, and no one knew where to turn to get the country on its feet again.

A man named Franklin Delano Roosevelt came on the scene. With help of strong Democrats like Joseph Kennedy, he was elected President of the United States in 1932. Joe hoped to become a member of Roosevelt's cabinet and serve as Secretary of the Treasury. When another man was named to the post, Joe was disappointed. President Roosevelt knew Joe was an intelligent and outspoken man. He later named him chairman of the new Securities and Exchange Commission, formed to help prevent another stock market crash.

Joe and Rose in 1934

Family picture in 1938

The years passed, the children grew, and life continued to be busy, full, and happy. In 1936, an important visitor named Eugenio Cardinal Pacelli, who was visiting the country, stopped at the Kennedy home for tea. He was one of the highest figures in the Catholic Church, and the Kennedys were most honored to have him as a guest. Teddy, then four years old, sat on his lap and was wide eyed as he played with the large jeweled cross worn by the Cardinal.

Joe welcoming his family to England

When the United States Ambassador to England resigned his post in 1938, President Roosevelt asked his good friend, Joe Kennedy, if he would take over the job of Ambassador to the Court of St. James. The position was very important, and Joe felt proud when he accepted.

Of course it meant that Joe and the family had to move to England. That was no easy matter because the children were scattered at various schools and colleges. But in March of 1938, the Kennedys arrived in London and took the country by storm. The English people immediately welcomed them with warmth and love.

Kathleen, Rose, and Rosemary before they were presented to King and Queen

**Attending a ball in honor of the
King and Queen of England, 1938**

Newspapers began to cover everything they did. The British seemed to be totally interested in the charming family. Bobby, age thirteen, and Teddy, age six, along with Kathleen, age twenty, joined their parents at the Ambassador's residence. The four girls, Eunice, Pat, Jean, and Rosemary, attended boarding schools near London. Rosemary's was a special school for slow learners. Joe Jr. and Jack were at Harvard. Somehow life remained somewhat normal.

Part of the ceremony of welcome to England included a presentation to King George VI and Queen Elizabeth of England, parents of the present Queen. Rose describes the event as one of the most memorable of her life. She and Joe also spent a weekend at Windsor Castle as guests of the King and Queen.

Eugenio Pacelli, who had been their guest, was elected pope in 1939. President Roosevelt asked the Kennedys to officially represent the United States at the coronation because they were an outstanding Catholic family.

At a party given at the American Embassy in 1939 are, left to right, Mrs. Rose Kennedy, King George VI, Queen Elizabeth, and Ambassador Kennedy

Ice skating in Switzerland in 1939 were Jean, 10, Rose, and Teddy, 7

**The Kennedy family at the Vatican after meeting
with the new Pope Pius XII**

Photographs have recorded the historic event of March
12, 1939. They show the entire family, except for Joe Jr.,
flanked by Papal Guards. The women wore black dresses
and veils. Jean, the youngest girl, wore a white dress and
veil. They were received in a private audience by the new
Pope Pius XII.

Twelve years later, Pius XII named Rose a Papal
Countess for her ''exemplary motherhood and many
charitable works.'' She was the only woman ever to be so
honored by Pope Pius XII.

The years in England were glamorous and
unforgettable, but war clouds were looming on the
horizon, foreshadowing terrible things to come.

26

4

The Price of War

Hitler was making demands and pushing the world to the brink of war. The United States and England had to decide whether he could be appeased or whether war had to come. Another question was whether the United States should get involved if war broke out.

As days passed and Hitler invaded Czechoslovakia, people lost hope. Hitler was a dictator and probably would never stop short of English shores in his lust for power. The situation in England was so historic and momentous that Joe Sr. called Jack to England from Harvard. Later Jack, who had closely watched the developments, wrote a masterpiece, **Why England Slept**, describing the last period before the great war.

When the Nazi armies invaded Poland, England had no choice but to declare war on Germany. The Kennedys made the choice to return to the States. Joe, of course, remained behind to attend high level discussions and meetings. Rosemary also remained at her special school on the English countryside.

Joseph, Kathleen, and John Kennedy go to House of Commons as Parliament decided on action which took the country into war

With the family on both sides of the ocean, letters flew back and forth. The war brought with it new decisions and directions to be taken. Joe Jr. decided to go into training as a Navy flier. Jack, having failed his first physical examination, exercised until he was in condition to be also accepted in the Navy. Kathleen, not to be outdone by her two older brothers, returned to England to work as a Red Cross nurse volunteer.

By 1941, the Kennedys had to face the fact that Rosemary, their oldest daughter, was mentally retarded and needed more care than they could give her. She was slow in learning to take care of herself. She demanded much attention and frequently there were tantrums. As much as her parents wanted to keep her in the family setting, they made the very painful decision to put her under the care of the Sisters of St. Coletta in Jefferson, Wisconsin. The sisters were specially trained to care for the mentally retarded. To this day Rosemary lives happily in a house there with a private car and driver. Her mother and family visit her often.

After completing his special training, John was put in command of a boat called the PT-109. When a Japanese submarine sliced the boat in two, John swam many miles with a sailor on his injured back to bring about a heroic rescue.

**Honey Fitz's 77th birthday celebration —
With him are his wife, his daughter Rose,
and his son-in-law, Joseph Kennedy**

Joe, the oldest son and favorite of his father, the son most active in politics, the one who had openly declared his intention of becoming the first Catholic president, was flying missions in Europe near the end of World War II.

At the same time Kathleen found herself romantically linked to Billy Cavendish, Marquis of Hartington, whose ancestors were pillars of the Church of England. Kathleen and her parents knew she could never marry him in the Catholic Church. Their differences in religion seemed to make marriage out of the question. Neither Billy nor Kathleen wanted to give up their own religions. After much pain and indecision, Kathleen decided to follow her heart. Her big brother Joe encouraged her decision. While on leave, he gave her away in a small court house marriage ceremony attended by only a few members of Billy's family and himself. The date was May 6, 1944.

Rose suffered heartbreak because she knew of Kathleen's love for Billy. She also knew and believed in the laws of her church.

The new bride and groom had just a few days together before Billy returned to the war front. Kathleen returned to the States for a visit with her parents. She was welcomed with tenderness and understanding.

Joe Jr., too, was soon back in action. When his required number of flights was completed, he volunteered for twenty more. The flights were dangerous. Their purpose was to protect Allied ground and sea forces. His successful completion of the second round made him one of the most experienced pilots in Europe.

Lord Hartington and Kathleen Kennedy were married in a short civil ceremony on May 6, 1944.

At that time he could have returned home to his family. But the Navy was seeking men for another very dangerous mission. Joe decided to volunteer. The new mission required getting a plane loaded with explosives into the air and under instrumental control of two other planes. The two pilots were to bail out to safety while the "mother" planes directed the explosive-laden plane to its crash landing in enemy territory, destroying the target thought to be an important rocket launching site.

Within one-half hour after its takeoff, the plane with Joseph Kennedy as one of the pilots exploded in midair. His body was never recovered.

Rose receives the Navy Cross won by her son, Joseph Jr. Looking on are her husband and children, Patricia, Edward, Robert, and Jean.

At Hyannis Port, the family was spending the day sailboat racing when two priests came to the door. The shocking and dreadful news that the oldest son and brother had been killed left the family silent and grief-stricken. Rose and Joe decided the family should be brave. Joe Jr. would have wanted it so. Joe Sr. told the kids to go ahead with their racing plans. Jack could not. He went for a long walk on the beach.

About one month later, in September, 1944, word came that Billy Cavendish, too, had been killed in Belgium. Kathleen returned to England to be with his family and to continue her Red Cross work.

No one realized then that the two deaths were but the beginning of a long series of tragedies to affect the lives of the Kennedys.

Life is for the Living

With Joe Jr. gone, Jack took up the political football and ran with it. He and others said Joe would not have wanted them to mope around. "Life is for the living."

Politics were in the Kennedy blood, and discussions stimulated further interest. No wonder, then, that by 1946 Jack decided to run for a Congressional seat held at one time by his grandfather, Honey Fitzgerald. The seat was easily won.

A business trip of Joe Sr. took him to Europe in 1948. He called Kathleen, who had made her home in England, to arrange a weekend together in Paris. On May 13, 1948, she excitedly boarded a small plane for a trip over the French Alps, thinking of the grand time she would have with her father.

Weather conditions were such that the pilots could not see the mountain until it was too late. Kathleen, the other passenger, and the crew were all killed.

Joe was at the foot of the mountain to identify his daughter's remains as she was brought down. Rose flew to England for the funeral, joining her husband to face another loss.

Jack with his mother and grandparents, campaigning
for a Congressional seat formerly held by his
grandfather, 1946

In 1952 a Senate seat fell vacant, so Jack set his cap for
that. But his opponent was Henry Cabot Lodge of the old
established Protestant Boston family.

With her double-barrelled name of Fitzgerald and
Kennedy, Rose campaigned for her son. The Bostonians
remembered her from the days when she was often seen
with her father. Now, as a Gold Star mother, she had
special authority and received special affection from the
people. She seemed to genuinely care about those she
met.

''Those teas did us in,'' the Lodges eventually
reported. What they referred to was a series of tea parties
organized to get out the women's votes. In each part of the
district, teas were planned. Everyone was invited and told
to bring a friend. One or more Kennedy, Rose, Eunice,
Jean, Pat, or Jack, was always the star attraction and
drawing card. Rose had a natural ability to say just the
right thing to appeal to the women gathered informally.
She enjoyed every minute of it.

Some commented that she had a keen political mind,
and that, in another day, she might have been the
candidate.

"Those teas did us in." 1952

6 Chapter

Moments of Pride

By the 1950's, the family was grown, and Rose, then sixty years old, had time to travel and enjoy her freedom. She kept a daily schedule of attending Mass, swimming in the Atlantic, playing nine holes of golf, and taking an afternoon nap. The Kennedy ''clan'' grew larger as the children married and started their own families.

Rose, known as the expert in raising children and in writing notes, wrote many letters and scribbled bits of advice on bringing up children to help the new parents. After her fashion, the Kennedy women made index files part of their households.

She could not forget her children, Joe and Kathleen, and her heart ached to hear their voices; but the others filled the house with gaiety and laughter. Every guest at Hyannis Port was mercilessly involved in a game of touch ball on the lawn. It was a hearty game, taken seriously, and everyone was out to win. No half-hearted playing was allowed.

Bobby and Ethel's wedding, 1950

Rose and Jackie with Catherine Nenehy in 1953

Since his brother's death, John had quietly pondered the presidency. As 1960 approached, he made his decision. No one was surprised to hear him announce his intentions: "I'm going to run for president."

Rose was delighted. She knew he had a special way with people and his own ideas on how the country should be run. He took seriously the biblical quotation, "To whom much has been given, much will be expected."

Caroline's baptism, 1957

By 1960 the Kennedys had become one of the richest families in the country. Joe Sr. had built a huge fortune through his ability to invest and manage money. The love and togetherness of the Kennedys also made them rich. Their affection for each other gave them the strength to move out of their own worlds into the world of service to others.

The nomination of John Fitzerald Kennedy as the Democratic candidate came in Los Angeles. His mother was at his side.

The campaign trail was long and hard. Like his grandfather, John met with those who would not vote for him because he was a Catholic. Some believed the old tales that through the Kennedys the Pope would take over the country. These people wanted to keep him from the White House by electing Nixon, the Republican candidate.

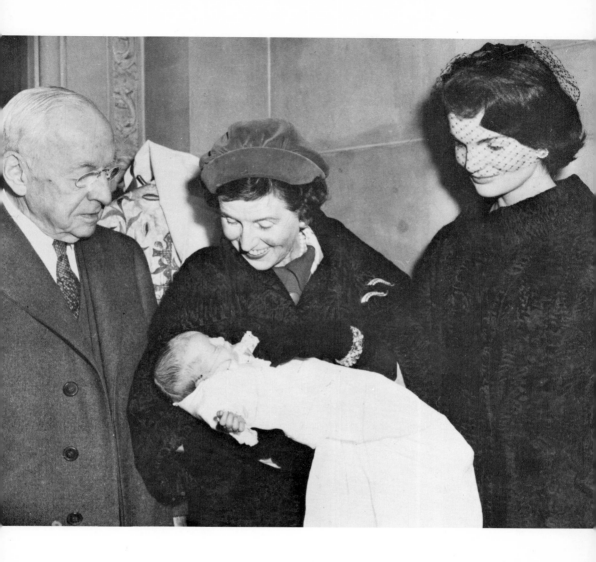

Rose hearing of Jack's nomination

The Kennedys mustered their forces and seemed to be everywhere. Rose's own schedule was set up by the campaign directors. They knew where she would be of greatest help. She travelled to many states appealing to women voters. She talked in a homey way about her family.

Up until the day of the election, no one knew for sure who would be elected.

The family gathered at Hyannis Port to await the results of the election. As the votes kept coming in, Nixon was reported to be ahead; then it was Jack who had the lead. By 3 a.m., the verdict seemed to be in. Jack left to return to his own home across the yard from his mother's and father's, accompanied by Secret Service men.

"Good night, Mr. President," Rose heard herself saying quietly.

The vote was close. Out of almost 69,000,000 votes cast, Jack received only 118,000 more than Richard Nixon. The family portrait of the Kennedys the day after the election showed mother Rose beaming as she sat with her beautiful family.

47

Standing proudly next to Jack

The Kennedy family the day after the election. Standing (l. to r.) are Ethel Kennedy, Steve Smith, Jean Smith, Senator John F. Kennedy, Robert Kennedy, Patricia Lawford, Sargent Shriver, Joan Kennedy, Peter Lawford. In the foreground (l. to r.) are Eunice Shriver, Mr. Kennedy, Mrs. Kennedy, Jacqueline Kennedy, and Edward Kennedy.

Rose welcomes Joe to Florida for the 1960 Christmas season.

When John visited President Eisenhower, both Rose and Joe saw the event televised. The two men met on the steps of the White House, shook hands, smiled for reporters, and went inside to chat. Both parents experienced a surge of pride. Finally it was indeed clear to them that their son was to be the next president.

One of the biggest blizzards in history engulfed Washington, D.C. as it prepared to receive its new president at the inauguration ceremony. Shivering along with everyone else, Rose and Joe Kennedy were warmed with love and pride as they listened to and applauded the new, young, vibrant president, their son, on whom the eyes of the nation were focused.

''Ask not what your country can do for you; ask what you can do for your country,'' he entreated all Americans.

As he gave his inaugural address, John remembered his parents and grandparents who had given examples of courage, judgment, honesty, and dedication. His ancestors had planted the seeds of glory.

At the inauguration ball, Rose was indeed a belle, a beautiful seventy-one year old woman who wore the same gown as when she was presented to the King and Queen of England about thirty-three years earlier.

7

Years of Camelot

People of the nation thought of John Fitzgerald Kennedy's presidential years as years of Camelot where all was sunshine, roses, and promise.

Most Friday afternoons, the presidential helicopter landed on the front lawn at Hyannis Port, carrying the First Family, Jack, Jacqueline, and their children, Caroline and John. They were welcomed by the handsome, cheering Kennedy clan. News reports seemed to indicate that indeed the days of Camelot had arrived.

Weekends were special as the Kennedys came from all over. Each family had a separate house in the neighborhood. The "Kennedy compound" was subjected to television and newspaper reporters, bombardment of tourists, and hordes of men sent to provide security.

Rose managed to keep sane while organizing the house for the weekend. A few basic rules were held over from earlier days: please be on time for meals and please put out the lights when not in use.

With Pope John XXIII, 1961

With the president in 1962 at a dinner at which the Kennedy Foundation made awards for research in the field of mental retardation

The happy days of Camelot remain in the heart of each Kennedy to this day.

Having built his financial fortune, Joe Sr. was more relaxed and happy than ever before. He loved his golf. On December 19, 1961, less than a year after he had been elected president, John said goodbye to his father after a short visit. Joe Sr. was then joined for a round of golf by his niece, Ann Gargan.

About the seventh hole, he felt a pain. He rode the golf cart back to his house, went to his room, and closed the door. He had suffered a serious stroke, one which left him paralyzed until his death eight years later.

Tragedy had left its mark on ''Camelot.''

Being interviewed by Charles Collingwood, October 30, 1963

8 Chapter

Woman of Strength

Probably everyone alive on November 22, 1963, remembers the horror of that day.

Rose had risen early, attended her usual daily Mass, and was resting when she heard a radio blaring loudly from the room of Dora, a maid. She came into the hall, somewhat irritated because she knew her husband needed all the rest he could get.

''The president has been shot!'' Dora sobbed.

Rose could not believe her ears. Her son had been at home during the previous week. He had convinced Jacqueline to join him on the political trip to Dallas. Confusion came upon Rose as she retreated to her room to quiet herself.

A few minutes later she appeared and gave instructions that her husband was not to hear the news until the children arrived. Minutes dragged on while the phone rang steadily bringing questions and news. There was little hope that Jack would live.

57

Ceremony at Arlington National Cemetery, November 25, 1963. At Jackie's right are Rose and Bobby.

Finally word came that he was dead, and the darkest
day of her life came upon Rose Kennedy. She could not
retreat, however. She knew that if she broke down, so
would her family. She kept herself in control while feeling
her heart would break.

Ted and Eunice arrived and immediately went in to see
their father.

''Jack has had an accident.''

Though no one could believe the terror of it all, the
children, in their own ways, tried to be positive and
comforting of each othér. They knew that Jack would have
wanted them to go on living instead of mourning him.

The weekend of the burial services found the tearful
people of the nation glued to their television sets.
Jacqueline, Rose, and all the Kennedys gave inspiration
through their strength and courage.

Little John saluted his father as the bier passed him.
Caroline understood only too well that her father would
never again scoop her into his arms for a hug.

Funeral scene

One can only begin to understand what the strength of a mother means to a family. But ''By their fruits you shall know them.'' The Kennedys picked themselves up to carry the torch which was their inheritance.

9 Chapter

Tragedy Again

And then there was Bobby, the second youngest son. Called ruthless by those who feared his work while attorney general in his brother's cabinet, Bobby was a loving husband to Ethel and father to ten children, with another one on the way.

No one was too surprised when he decided to run for president in 1968. As his brother John's closest friend, he knew the unfinished work before him and was determined to do what he could to get the United States out of the Vietnam War.

After winning the primary election in California, a most important state, he was cheered and applauded amid bedlam at the Ambassador Hotel in Los Angeles where he had made his headquarters.

Sitting in church praying for Bobby's recovery

Surrounded by secret service men on his way through a narrow kitchen passage, he was felled by a bullet which pierced the heart of the nation. Within forty-eight hours he was dead.

Could his mother help wondering what was to become of her family? One by one each was leaving her, the victims of the most senseless tragedies.

She journeyed to New York City where her son's body lay in state at St. Patrick's Cathedral, the old church in the center of the city. She spent the night in prayerful vigil, drawing courage from the Mother of Sorrows who saw her beloved son killed almost 2000 years earlier.

She believed that Bobby, Jack, Joe, and Kathleen lived, and that they would all be together again some day. She believed God knew what He was doing with her and her family, and she tried to accept His will with peace. But the terror, the heartache, and the uselessness of Bobby's death were almost too much to bear.

63

Leaving St. Patrick's Cathedral after Bobby's funeral. With Rose is Robert F. Kennedy, Jr.

10 Chapter

Love Greater than Life

Mr. Kennedy's condition worsened. His niece, Ann Gargan, was always at his side. His stroke took away his ability to talk and walk, but he kept a sharp mind and an ablity to understand what was said to him. He could also sense the unspoken messages.

He was always on Rose's mind, no matter where she was or what she was doing.

''I love him more than life itself,'' she once said, and the devoted love kept her near him. They would eat all their meals together, and she would read to him letters and magazine articles which she knew to be of interest.

Joe began to lose his eyesight and with it one of his favorite pastimes and greatest pleasures, television. Rose found it hard to see him suffer. She remembered his energy, his ambition, his handsomeness, his spirit, his heart which showed tenderness to her and the children, and his mind which would never quit working. She wondered how much longer he could live in his condition.

With John at his inauguration, 1961

With Kathleen on the Queen Mary, 1945

On November 18, 1969, surrounded by his wife and children who were called home to be at his bedside, he died.

He had lived a full life and had seen his son as the first Catholic president of the country he deeply loved. He had seen his children reap the benefits of his efforts to free them from money worries so they could be of service to others. He left the greatest part of his estate to the Joseph P. Kennedy Jr. Foundation to aid the mentally retarded.

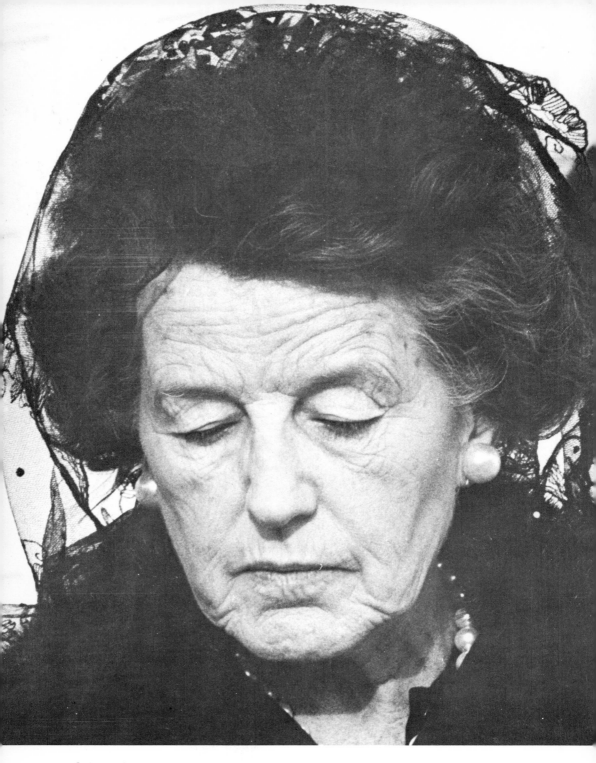

Solemn-faced Rose leaves church after attending Mass. Her husband had died the day before.

No Time
for Tears

Dag Hammerskjold once wrote that thinking about the past and dreaming about the future can neither bring back the past nor fulfill one's dreams. What is important is how one lives the here and now.

Determined to be a burden to none, Rose Kennedy, slim, beautiful, sparkling, quick, and fashionable, lives a peaceful and purposeful life.

Laughing with Joan and Ted

Dedicating JFK's birthplace

Raising money for retarded people

Working with the retarded

Campaigning for Ted with Joseph Kennedy, III, 1970

Sailing

Celebrating Caroline's graduation

Her autobiography **Times to Remember** has been
published. All money from the sale of the book will go to a
foundation for the mentally retarded. Rose is continually
aware of the on-going needs of retarded people.

One of her favorite works is the Joseph P. Kennedy
Jr. Foundation which has been a major force in improving
attitudes about the mentally retarded. Where shame and
secrecy once surrounded the retarded family member,
openness and help now prevail. The Kennedys sponsor
summer camps for the retarded, and the grandchildren
volunteer their time. By giving individual attention to
someone learning to throw a ball, for example, the
volunteer hastens that person's development and pride in
himself.

Rose especially loves these words from the Book of Ecclesiastes:

There is a season for everything, and a time for every
purpose under heaven.
A time for giving birth,
a time for dying;
a time for tears,
a time for laughter;
a time for mourning,
a time for dancing.
A time for embracing,
and a time to refrain from embracing.

She has seen the seasons of her life come and go. Today she has time to reflect. She cannot forget the tragedies, but she chooses to remember the good times of the past and experience the good times of the present.

With her faith and love, she has no time for tears.

CAROL BAUER CHURCH is a graduate of the College of St. Catherine in St. Paul, Minnesota. She is a former school teacher and lives with her husband Jim and daughter Laura. She is currently working on additional titles for the **Focus on Famous Women Series**.

DATE DUE

MAY 9 1986			
9 198? MAY 0 2 1995			
FEB 2 3 1990			
Surgcit			
FEB 1 0 1995			
FEB 1 0 1996			